THE LEISURE CLASS IN AMERICA

This is a volume in the Arno Press collection

THE LEISURE CLASS IN AMERICA

Advisory Editor
Leon Stein

A Note About This Volume

The son of a great publisher, Ralph Pulitzer (1879-1939) presents a devastating picture of the leaders of "society" in his day. He finds them lacking in grace and good taste and caustically describes their ritual conduct at The Dinner, The Opera, The Dance, etc. In the *Bookman*, Frank Crowninshield acknowledged the author's wit while bewailing his bitterness. "It is a thousand pities," he wrote, "that Mr. Pulitzer could not have coupled in this extraordinary little book good nature with satire and sympathy with cleverness. His wit is altogether too good to be wasted on so exaggerated and so bitter a book."

See last pages of this volume for a complete list of titles.

New York Society
On Parade

RALPH PULITZER

ARNO PRESS

A New York Times Company

New York / 1975

E
161
.L4P8
Cop 2

Fordham University
LIBRARY
AT
LINCOLN CENTER
New York, N. Y.

Reprint Edition 1975 by Arno Press Inc.

Reprinted from a copy in
 The Newark Public Library

THE LEISURE CLASS IN AMERICA
ISBN for complete set: 0-405-06900-6
See last pages of this volume for titles.

Manufactured in the United States of America

———•⟨∞⟩•———

Library of Congress Cataloging in Publication Data

Pulitzer, Ralph, 1879-1939.
  New York society on parade.

  (The Leisure class in America)
  Reprint of the 1910 ed. published by Harper, New York.
  1. New York (City)--Social life and customs. 2. Upper classes--New York (City) I. Title. II. Series.
HN80.N5P8 1975   309.1'747'1   75-1866
ISBN 0-405-06932-4

New York Society on Parade

[See page 114.

UNITED IN THE HOLY BONDS OF WALTZ OR TWO-STEP

New York Society
On Parade

RALPH PULITZER

WITH ILLUSTRATIONS BY
HOWARD CHANDLER CHRISTY

HARPER & BROTHERS PUBLISHERS
NEW YORK AND LONDON
M C M X

Copyright, 1910, by HARPER & BROTHERS

All rights reserved

Published February, 1910
Printed in the United States of America

ILLUSTRATIONS

UNITED IN THE HOLY BONDS OF WALTZ OR TWO-STEP	*Frontispiece*	
THE LADIES LEAVE THE STRICKEN FIELD	*Facing p.*	30
THEIR MINDS GROPE TOWARD ONE ANOTHER ALONG A TENUOUS BRIDGE OF WORDS	"	44
THE "HORSE-SHOE" AT ITS BEST	"	68
A YOUNG MAN OF EXCELLENT FAMILY BUT NO FORTUNE, AND—OF NO PROSPECTS	"	72
APPRAISED FOR THE BEAUTY OF THEIR FACES OR THE BOUNTY OF THEIR FAMILIES	"	114
REST AND REFRESHMENT AWAIT AT THE SUPPER-TABLES BELOW	"	118
AT SUPPER A SUPERFICIAL FAMILIARITY EXISTS	"	212

NEW YORK SOCIETY ON PARADE

NEW YORK SOCIETY ON PARADE

IN European nations "Society" is the formal intercourse between members of the upper class—the aristocracy.

With these aristocracies Society is an intermittent condition created by the temporary meeting of persons of permanent rank—persons who possessed their rank before their association made Society, and retain it after their separation for the time being ends Society.

If every member of the upper class in Europe simultaneously entered upon the life of a recluse for one year, European Society would for that year cease to exist. But at the year's end when these men and women again came together in formal reunions, and thus again formed "Society," they would all, or practically all, possess the same membership of their upper class, and would each occupy the identical relative position in their Society as before their year's isolation.

If, however, the same catastrophe overtook New York, short indeed would be the roster of those families which could emerge with positions undisturbed and prestige unshaken, still standing like fashionable monoliths amid the rack and ruin.

For while European Society consists of a deep mill-pond of assured position with a froth of probationary parvenus, New York Society consists of a whirlpool of tentative novices with a sediment of permanent members.

Instead, indeed, of having an aristocracy whose caste is beyond question and beyond change and whose mutual hospitalities constitute Society, New York has an "Aristocracy" whose elevation is largely artificial, whose membership is largely arbitrary, and whose existence vitally depends upon those activities which are known as social functions. In other words, while in Europe the mutual entertainments of an inherently stable upper class create Society, in New York the constant contortions of Society are indispensable to create and maintain a precarious upper class; while in Europe the pleasures of Society are among the prerogatives of rank, in New York the pleasure of "rank" is the inducement to Society.

NEW YORK SOCIETY ON PARADE

The contrast between the two species of Society is precisely the contrast between the amateur athlete who exercises for his amusement and the professional athlete who exercises for a living.

Thus in New York beneath the frivolity and flippancy with which Society bedizzens itself, like the paint and tights in which a chorus girl must do her work, that Society is transacting deadly earnest business.

There is, no doubt, much spontaneous pleasure incidental to this business—débutantes may dance, gliding and colliding with unalloyed ecstasy; gourmets may gormandize, and tipplers tipple, taking unreservedly what the gods give them. But, ever present, all-pervading, gleaming in the glossy floor, pulsating in the rhythmic music, flavoring the subtle sauce, bubbling in the foaming glass, re-echoing through the banal conversation, is the spirit of desperate and dogged travail of those who, to the cause of "class," are devoting their lives, their fortunes, and their sacred honor.

All that may be said about these men and women is said of them in their official capacity as members of "Society." In whatever private lives they lead they are neither under observation nor criticism. As individuals in the company of their families or friends, in their informal hospitalities and amusements, many of the women and most of the men are kindly unaffected human beings, performing normal functions from natural motives, liking each other without premeditation, disliking each other without deliberation, cultivating each other instinctively, cutting each other impulsively, enjoying themselves, and boring themselves with equal spontaneity; eating their daily cake a trifle more lightly than their less favored fellow citizens earn their daily bread, but differing from these latter much less than do such classes in other nations. While they live their lives of private domesticity or of private diversion, any praise or censure levelled at them would be merely an impertinence levelled at the human nature of the human race. But when the call-boy runs the rounds, and most of these same gentlemen and ladies strut or scuttle from their private dressing-rooms to form their tableaux on the public stage, and go through all the mummery of mimes, plodding or pirouetting through the rôles assigned them by the playwright Vanity, then in their professional degree they become fair game for any philosopher or fool.

NEW YORK SOCIETY ON PARADE

We have seen the fundamental distinction between a European upper class which finds in Society the relaxation from its responsibilities or the pastime of its leisure, and those citizens of New York who make of Society a responsibility from which there is no relaxation, a pastime from which there is no leisure.

If we bear this distinction in mind we shall be able to study New York Society with some degree of intelligent sympathy, if not of emotional compassion. For the struggle for self-preservation of even the humblest living things is no laughing matter.

I

THE DINNER

THE dinner is probably the formal entertainment in which New York Society shows to the best attainable advantage.

It is true that the conditions are not such as to make possible those intellectual pleasures which are supposed to be a paramount element of the ideal dinner. Yet the sympathetic and collective enjoyment by numerous guests of adroitly prepared food and judiciously laid wine can surely pass muster as an entirely appropriate object for a social congregation. And as wealth alone is needed to provide superlative dishes and vintages through the agencies of a deft *chef* and a discriminating wine agent, and as relatively little training is needed to equip nervously intelligent palates with a capacity for critical appreciation, a dinner may be said to furnish more spontaneous pleasure to its participants than any other variety of formal entertainment, and therefore to possess the most legitimate reason for existence.

A formal dinner does not take place till half-past eight o'clock. This comparative lateness of the hour has numerous advantages. It gives the ladies time to rest in the late afternoon from the fatigue of their earlier duties before preparing for the responsibilities of the coming hours. It gives many who have not had quite so many duties to exhaust them, or who may have pusillanimously shirked those duties, a pleasant hour's play-time with their children, while others it gives a lucky moment in which to kiss their little ones a simultaneous good-morning and good-night. It gives them all an opportunity to resuscitate delicate appetites from the stupor in which afternoon tea has left them buried.

This dining hour also enables the majority of the younger men who have left work and Wall Street for their clubs between three and four o'clock, to keep themselves in fine physical condition by playing wholesome games of court-tennis, "squash," or racquets, or by betting on the wholesome games that other men are playing. It gives a chance to the small minority, principally lawyers, who are not in Wall Street and who work till six o'clock, to bathe and dress for dinner at their clubs instead of having to dress without a bath at their offices. These latter from among their scanty ranks generally furnish the only oases of intellect which blossom in society amid deserts of "brains" and mirages of mentality. So any hour of dining which will tend to lure these ioslated intellects into leavening Society's batter of common sense and good nature is fortunate for the dinner and is rightly to be encouraged.

This hour has a further advantage in permitting these young men, after their exercise, their betting, and their bathing have been accomplished, and all whom wedlock has not forced to dress at home, are clad for the impending occasion, to sit at ease with their more elderly fellow guests-to-be, and possess themselves, in slow luxurious gulps, of the ardent mellowness of successive cocktails. An accurate accumulation of these, discreetly adapted to each participant's just requirements, will markedly aid the coming function's brilliance. For these stimulating compounds not only sharply increase the appetite, thus enhancing powers of enjoying the material ingredients of even the most formal dinner, but at the same time they encourage to abnormal activity any mental powers which may lie within their reach. They cannot change a brain into an intellect, it is true, but they can flick it into such a brisk brain that it may give a very creditable imitation of an intellect. They cannot give it ideals, but they may give it enthusiasms; they cannot give it thought, but they may give it fancies; they cannot give it acquired knowledge, but they can give it improvised theories; they cannot give it wit, but they can give it jocularity.

These attributes, when added to the

natural alertness of intelligence which is the rule in American minds, may help to make the subsequent dinner pass amid a table talk so copious and so vivacious that it is a serious question whether it has not the right to rank among dinner conversations.

The scene of a formal dinner is becoming more and more exclusively confined to the region between Central Park and Park Avenue on the west and east, and Fiftieth Street and Eightieth Street on the south and north, as New York Society deserts its older habitations to concentrate in that locality.

A long strip of carpet winds its way from the front door across the sidewalk to the curb, sheltered by an awning and presided over by a groom whose function it is to open the doors of carriages and automobiles which possess no grooms of their own, and to summon these conveyances at the evening's end. He can also inform arrivals at what hour carriages are being ordered to return, and thus can give them an idea how early they may depart without rudeness if they are being bored, or how late they may stay on if they are being amused or are winning at bridge.

The guests generally begin to reach the seat of hospitality about ten minutes after the hour of invitation. Very frequently, however, an old-fashioned couple, who still live on Washington Square or in its vicinity, and who have decided to experiment with a taxi-cab as a far-sighted economy for such a distance, whirl up to their destination a good ten minutes before the appointed hour, and are doomed to spend those minutes in repeatedly circumvolving the city block on which their hosts reside, while the dial of their premature conveyance jumps spasmodically for every circumvolution. Frequently, too, the inmates of the next-door house (for not only is the mutual identity of neighbors occasionally known, but they are at times on terms of social intimacy) are the last to arrive, some thirty minutes late, in a paroxysm of apology and haste, as the result of too implicit a faith in proximity as an antidote to procrastination.

Between these two extremes of punctuality and lateness broughams, landaus, and limousines deposit their fashionable freight, while occasional couples walk over from beyond Park Avenue, where some of Society's least wealthy and most creditable members and nearly all of Society's horses dwell intermingled in thoroughbred harmony.

This, incidentally, is one of the most praiseworthy features of New York Society. Not that it locates its horses among its most creditable members, but that, being a Society chiefly created and preserved by money, it should be broad-minded enough to welcome cordially to its ranks so many persons of limited means.

As the guests enter the house the ladies are ushered into one cloak-room and the men into another. The men go through the simple operation of taking off their overcoats and hats and getting a check by which to reclaim them. They are also handed a little stiff envelope containing a card which each man draws forth as gingerly as he would the fifth card to four of a suit. They then issue from their cloak-room, and each of them who accompanies a lady stands, a monument of expectant patience, gazing wistfully at the door behind which the mysteries are taking place on whose accomplishment he waits. When the object of his patience finally radiates his view he follows her, generally up an imposing sweep of stairs, intently scrutinizing the edge of her train upon which Nemesis is hounding him to place his foot. Near the head of the staircase they find the hostess surrounded by a bevy of Beau Brummels. As they approach, the most distinguished-looking of these, stepping forward, enunciates their names in tones of great volume and distinctness, and the mistress of the house welcomes them with that indelible smile which hostesses share exclusively with coiffeurs' models and with Christian martyrs. They then mingle with the guests who have preceded them, the men, if they know the ladies whose names are on their cards, painstakingly avoiding them till it is time to take them in to dinner, and, if they by chance do not know them, desperately striving to discover their identity; the ladies suffering themselves to be avoided and ultimately discovered with a suavity that veils the interest they feel in this marriage in miniature. For, after all, a dinner spent between two bores may seem as infinite in alternating dulness as a life spent between two husbands, and there is no Dakota for the dinner guest.

Then the butler, with a remarkable mixture of calculation and intuition, knows that the latest arrivals are indeed the last, and, with unostentatious irony, announces to the hostess the readiness of that dinner which, during the past half-hour, has budded, blossomed, and all but withered, saved only by the frantic ministrations of a heroic *chef* and his devoted kitchen maids.

The prandial procession forms and gracefully wends its way into the dining-room, where those guests known by sight to the servants are quickly pointed to their places, while those not thus privileged wander about like lost and aimless spirits, till finally, by a prolonged process of elimination, they find and sink into their proper seats.

The first fifteen minutes of the dinner are generally its best. For hunger is essentially a spontaneous emotion: its gratification is inevitably a natural operation. It is impossible to crave food with any ulterior design, it is impossible to eat food with any complex calculation. The animal appetite does not lend itself to formality: Society shares it with the dumb brutes and the lower classes.

NEW YORK SOCIETY ON PARADE

Dowager or débutante, captain of industry or floor broker, while they still their hunger they are to that extent sincere. And as, fortunately, the majority of the guests are hungry during the first quarter of an hour of dinner, an atmosphere of sincerity prevails about the table.

The oysters come and succulently vanish; the soup steams fragrantly and softly gurgles to oblivion; the fish leaves but a skeleton behind. And all this while frank pleasure permeates the Gothic dining-room.

Some scattered exceptions among the guests, the victims of infirmities of body or afflictions of temperament, wonder whether the tapestries upon the walls are really Gobelins; whether the golden candelabra on the table were wedding-presents; whether the mauve satin showing through the lace insertions of the tablecloth is vulgar or fashionable; whether the orchestra which is murmuring from the hall is Sherry's or Franko's. The hostess racks her brain beneath her smiles to decide whether there are enough of these exceptions present to jeopardize her entertainment's success.

But the majority of the guests are devoting themselves to their uncomplicated pleasures, enjoying these pleasures with the grace of breeding or of manners which saves them from all taint of gluttony, sustaining the conversation in somewhat automatic intermezzos that fill the leisure moments between the courses, and, while these early courses hold the stage, continuing their discourse in intermittent obligatos, a concession by nature to civilization, by the palate to the tongue.

But now the supreme moments of the

dinner are done, for with the entrée comes the exit of the polite but whole-souled self-abandonment of diners to dinner.

Hunger gives way to fastidiousness, unreasoning pleasure to analyzing appreciation. Part of the enjoyment that is to come is, no doubt, still legitimate, for when men and women are formally asked to an elaborate dinner they have the right to enjoy the manner of the cooking as well as the matter of the cooked.

But as earnest joy in the essence of food fades into a decadent appreciation of the form and technique of dishes, so the crude but stimulating atmosphere of the genuine evaporates, and there comes wafting through the dining-room the soft and subtle haze of artifice.

For, as the guests eat less and taste more, they remember more vividly where they are. The tapestries emerge from the walls, the golden candelabra grow like mango plants, the mauve satin blazes up through the lace insertions, each man's neighbors develop attributes of gratifying beauty or of disappointing ugliness. Each woman's dress grows even more enviable or more pitiable to the eyes of other women than it was before the beginning of dinner interrupted mutual observations. The hostess's new emerald pendant becomes a token of marital devotion or a provocation to absolute divorce. The ugly financier may drop a valuable hint on market tendencies if the beautiful young matron is sympathetic enough. The bright young Westerner may get the entrée to the fat old lady's drawing-room if he is amusing enough. The rising architect may get his plans accepted by the irascible-looking man if he can sufficiently interest the latter's daughter in the æsthetic possibilities of tenement-houses. The effeminate youth may be taken for years older than he is if he can talk cynically enough to the horsy-looking girl. The wistful débutante may catch the point of the risqué story, which her left-hand neighbor is telling the mournful lady on his farther side, if she can listen acutely enough with one ear while bending the other pensively to the remarks of the eloquent young rector on her right.

Course follows course in infinite variety. The dinner becomes a brilliant culinary vaudeville, where attraction on attraction kaleidoscopically flits in swift review, and manners, alas! forbid a curtain-call. The servants cease from waiting on the guests and gradually become so many prestidigitators, palming the most promising plates beneath their exasperated victims' very eyes, proving, with tantalizing success, that the quickness of the hand deceives the palate.

The general animation grows and spreads infectiously. The hostess, feeling that from her point of view the dinner has passed its danger-point and is on the highroad to success, permits herself to cease from smiling. Men, gazing alternately into the liquid shallows of sparkling eyes and twinkling champagne-glasses, feel their beings bursting with noble thoughts, novel theories, or brilliant wit, only waiting their expression in flights of an eloquence which has also been vouchsafed them. Women feel themselves glow with a more radiant loveliness, tingle with a more irresistible magnetism, fit their gowns with a snugger perfection—become, in short, more wholly adapted to be the inspiration of any man who needs one.

But thoughts, theories, and wit, loveliness, magnetism, and inspiration are not sufficient unto themselves as hunger was. If the thoughts would be content with comprehension, the theories with acceptance, the wit with appreciation, the loveliness with admiration, the magnetism with domination, as hunger is satisfied with its appeasement, the dinner would still have the beauty of sincerity even if all these auto-attributes were merely imaginary.

But they are not thus satisfied. For behind the loveliness lurk the Wall Street tips, behind the theory lurks the tenement-house, behind the wit lurks the exclusive invitation, behind the inspiration lurks the risqué story. And behind most of the other attributes which grow and flourish as the dinner advances stretch as both their objects and their instigations the threads of a complex web of artificial ideals, artificial ambitions, artificial apprehensions, artificial resentments, running all the gamut of the sentiments of an unreal existence from artificial triumph to artificial despair.

As the animation grows, the flow of talk breaks into a cataract of conversation. This dashes itself from topic to topic, but boils chiefly round the subject of what was done yesterday, what is planned for tomorrow, what common friends are doing and are saying. Plays are touched on, but acting is ignored; operas are discussed, but only for the personal performances of celebrated singers, not for the music of the operas themselves. Politics are discussed only in so far as they affect the Stock Exchange or the race-track. Politicians are, of course, beneath discussion, save in the rare cases of male members of Society who have answered the call for gentlemen to enter politics for their purification, and who have invariably turned out the most pointedly practical politicians of the lot. Painting is discussed only to the extent of the latest fashionable foreign artist's portrait of the latest fashionable native Society woman. Literature is less fortunate, being considerably talked about in the shape of the latest fiction; but all the talk confines itself to the plot and character; the style is left severely to itself. Science is discussed only as represented by the merits of competing types of automobiles. Statesmanship figures in the conversation only as manifested in the iniquities of a tariff system which makes possible the New York customs inspection; the most effective methods of nullifying this system being also touched on.

It would be very unfair, however, to suppose that the manner of all this talk is dull because the subjects are superficial. On the contrary, the spirit of the conversation is one of brightness, quick-wittedness, keenness of perception, shrewdness of conclusion. It is almost as if native intelligence wished to prove (and came remarkably near proving) how independent it could afford to be of substantial knowledge and of cultivated interests.

There are, of course, men and women at almost every large dinner who are exceptions to these rules. Some distinguished bankers are interested and expert in matters of art, many prominent lawyers follow with keen interest the developments of public affairs, some women have a deep love and technical knowledge of music, and, more rarely, of painting. Some women are hard and intelligent workers in the fields of practical philanthropy.

But any of these who may be at such formal dinners are almost sure to be few and far between; they are apt to find themselves isolated from any kindred natures, flanked impermeably by amiable ignorance and politely veiled indifference. Thus this little incompatible minority can have no visible effect on the prevailing tone and temper of the assembly. They either mercifully drug their intellects, and, by the reflex actions of their brains, join in the mental rompings which surround them, or if, through lack of adaptability, they cannot play such parts, they sit like pedants, doctrinaires and bores, steeped in the dulness almost always displayed by depth when surrounded by superficiality.

THE LADIES LEAVE THE STRICKEN FIELD

Meanwhile the dinner has run its course, and, beneath the babel of tripping tongues, a curious suspense makes itself felt. It is the telepathic manœuvres of the hostess marshalling her feminine forces to rise and leave the stricken field for the tedious respite of the drawing-room. At this moment it would be of melancholy interest to know how many conversations cut short by this exodus have been of sufficient interest to cause in the conversers any disappointment at the interruption, or any intention to pursue the subject at the next opportunity.

The ladies glide into the drawing-room, the men saunter into the library for their cigars and coffee. There the host is apt to be momentarily embarrassed by one or more among his guests who, with misguided politeness, do not content themselves with admiring the masters on the walls, but ask him their names and even the subjects of their portraits.

The general conversation, however, quickly turns into a safer and more congenial channel and sweeps the inconvenient questioners along with it. The guests luxuriously puff their admirable cigars whose smoke flows forth as smooth as ever tape from ticker, and in the eddying clouds, with comfortably half-shut eyes or glances feverishly bright, men trace the shapes of the fluctuating fortunes which "The Street" has brought to them that day.

The market is the one inspiration that can transmute general loquacity into general eloquence. It is not merely that the future of a stock is like the future of the soul, a subject on which any one man's guess is as tenable as any other man's theory. But practically every man present has learned his stock quotations at his mother's knee. He knows "The Street," its traditions, its practices, its aspirations, its whole history, a great deal better than he knows the history of his country.

He could narrate the story of Black Friday far more minutely and infinitely more correctly than he could the story of Gettysburg. He could reel off the list of great Wall Street manipulators from the first down to present company far more glibly than he could the list of the Presidents of the United States. He could name the precise capitalization of any great corporation a great deal more readily than he could the exact number of Presidential electors of his own State.

And he who can do all this is not alone the fortunate one who has been ordained to financial orders, who is doing the work of the elect on the floor of the holy of holies, who is preaching the prospectus among them who sit in darkness, or performing modern miracles in the name of Mammon, turning water into capital, and making undigested securities fall manna-like from the skyey heights of high finance.

But the other men present, whose professions or business have no connection with the science of exploiting the elevation or depression of stocks, engross themselves in it as an avocation. If fate forbids them to devote to it their labors as experts and specialists they can at least devote their leisure as gifted dilettantes, amateur virtuosos, to this most artful of the arts. Thus it is that when Wall Street becomes the topic of conversation a unique atmosphere at once prevails.

NEW YORK SOCIETY ON PARADE

Doctor, lawyer, architect, real-estate owner, railroad president, manufacturer, and mine-owner mingle indistinguishably with banker, broker, speculator, promoter. A tone of fervor makes the voices ring. Faith kindles eyes, devotion lights up faces. The eloquence of earnestness breaks forth, tenderly investing with the radiance of romance the most sordid puts and calls, and longs and shorts, and margins and corners, and coverings and takings of profits.

There are, of course, exceptions here again. Some bolder and less conventional minds, unswayed by the prevailing enthusiasm, soberly discuss the chances of next year's polo teams, analyze the fine points of yesterday's racquet finals, or argue with bewildering technicality and ignorance the rival merits of the high-tension and the low-tension magneto.

NEW YORK SOCIETY ON PARADE

And in one corner a slightly over-stimulated old financier is telling two young men just out of college how he once knew Lincoln well, despite his wretched manners; and they are listening with polite embarrassment to this unsought revelation of a youthful indiscretion.

Of course, too, there may be present a fine old judge who is quoting Horace to a college president; the weazened banker may be maintaining to the florid young broker that Sir Philip Francis could not have written the Junius letters, the street-railway president may be discoursing to the copper-mine owner on the possibilities of the five-time in which that movement in Tschaikowski's sixth symphony was composed; the real-estate owner may be discussing with the Standard Oil capitalist the proofs that George Bancroft wrote President Johnson's first message to Congress.

Any or all of these phenomena might conceivably take place in the smoke-hazed library. But they would be exceptional and not typical as is the Wall Street pæan which sounds its rich harmonies through the handsome room.

And yet this zealous talk which rises and falls like its mutable subject bears its share in the dinner's real success. For it is the sincere and unstudied enjoyment of members of a commercial Society, or perhaps rather of a Society which has become too complex to adhere to crude commercialism, and therefore has become addicted to the more polished development of commercialism concealed in speculation—just as Elizabethan Society, which would have scorned to sail the seas in merchantmen, delighted to find glory and doubloon in the lucrative depredations of the gentlemen adventurers.

So this mercenary talk represents what they have of enthusiasm or of aspirations. It is "a poor thing but" their own. The portion of the evening devoted to it is at least clean of all artificiality. They utilize one another's society to discuss the matter which monopolizes their individual and social interest. What more legitimate object could a social gathering serve?

But now the host arises, and throwing the stump of his cigar into the blazing fire, starts resolutely for the door. A suppressed moan vibrates from those who have found such solace in their first cigar that they have just begun a second one. But waste has ever been the handmaid of chivalry; so cherished Invincibles, in the full flush of life and beauty, are consigned, living, to the flames, or are left to meet a malodorous death upon the scattered ash-trays, while their executioners troop back to join the ladies.

These have been spending their time with liqueurs, coffee, cigarettes, and one another—four stimulants the last three of which they are apt to abuse. They have not only talked dresses and babies while scrutinizing one another zealously for anything new, but some have also discussed the domestic labor problems of the day. Those of them who have only just met converse with courteous caution, choosing as their text such trivial and non-committal subjects as the latest matinée to which they have both been, and which ones of their most creditable acquaintances they saw there; how delightful the dance was night before last, and how much they are looking forward to the musicale day after to-morrow; how unbecoming mourning is to one common acquaintance, and how becoming divorce has been to another; what an exquisite house this is, and what a delicious dinner they have just had.

Those who know one another somewhat better say charming things about one another's fascinating little children, and ask one another questions about the nationality of their nurses and the nature of their nourishments.

Those whose acquaintance is verging on friendship talk clothes: the hopeless fashion in hats just coming in, yet how, of course, one will have to wear them; how expensive one's dressmaker is becoming, who was once so reasonable; what stunning models another dressmaker has who has just moved to Fifth Avenue. They inform one another of the latest dressmaker in Paris to whom respectable women are just beginning to go. They give one another addresses in Paris where they say one can get such pretty things so ridiculously cheap; but they do not give one another the addresses where they actually do get such pretty things ridiculously cheap. Those they keep sacredly to themselves for fear of spoiling the shop with too much custom.

Those who are intimate friends, besides talking children and clothes, seal the bonds of this intimacy by plunging sorrowfully into the gloom of the servant question. For there is no royal road to peace with servants, nor is there any public highway, either. Millions and housekeepers may stave off the doom, as millions and doctors may stave off death; but the servant will go and the undertaker will come, alike inexorable. So the most lavish hostess and the most thrifty housewife among the guests share the dreadful interest in the kitchen, the pantry, and the servants' hall; and together those of them who are bosom friends pore over the problems of feuds between housekeepers and butlers, of feuds between butlers and parlor maids, of feuds between housemaids and ladies' maids; of ruinous commissions to *chefs* or cooks; of chauffeurs who will not eat with mere servants; of nurses who ring the bell for pressing needs five times an hour; of decorative footmen ruined by drink.

These are but a few of the tribulations which are poured into the ears of trusted friends, and which these friends strive to mitigate with tender sympathy and adroit advice.

Thus they sit and chat in nervous silken grace, fingering their cigarettes, whose

NEW YORK SOCIETY ON PARADE

incense puffs from curving lip or chiselled nostrils as delicate as any innuendo.

To the men, shuffling in through the wide doorway, they present a formidable aspect and an apparently impregnable solidarity. But they quickly break up with their assailants into scattered couples and quartets.

Now will come the supreme test of the evening's higher success. These men and women have in the first part of the dinner enjoyed one another's society in the sympathy of a common appetite which precluded more delicate affinities. Throughout the rest of dinner their social intercourse was continued with the aids and accessories of a rapid and varied sequence of dishes. After dinner the men had their cigars and Wall Street, the women their cigarettes and clothes, as habits to occupy their attentions. But now they sit face to face, mind to mind, with neither food, nor cooking, nor dress, nor stocks to serve as distractions and allies to their conversation. They sit in the regions of pure thought. Will their minds, groping toward one another along a tenuous bridge of words, meet and find companionship in mutuality of mental interest? Will their tastes in common soar from oysters to authors, from artichokes to architecture, from canvas-backs to composers, from pease to poetry? Or will their minds, like babies walking without furniture, toddle toward one another, meet in dizzy contact, and, having fallen painfully to earth, crawl sniffling piteously back to their respective nurseries?

No one will ever know. For at this moment when Opportunity stands smiling inscrutably with hands behind her, holding in either palm success or failure, there

THEIR MINDS GROPE TOWARD ONE ANOTHER ALONG A TENUOUS BRIDGE OF WORDS

comes a strident twanging, and through the door at one end of the drawing-room march negro minstrels, fortune-tellers, mind-readers, provided to amuse the guests so that they need not face the ordeal of interesting one another.

With muffled exclamations of relief they for the most part sink on rows of chairs, permitting their minds, agitated by the prospect of aimless activity, to relapse into the receptive attitude of being entertained.

A goodly number, however (whose brains, holding possibilities of better things, crave exercise without exertion), withdraw into a neighboring Adam *salon*, where small green tables with four chairs at each invite to games of bridge.

Seating themselves, these guests are soon engrossed in play, solemnly heedless of the flippant laughter and applause that echo intermittently from the adjoining room.

And now again the spirit of Sincerity, poor spirit which has been alternately entertained unawares and cruelly rebuffed during the evening's course, comes stealing in to lend her auspices alike to grand slam and revoke.

For once again these members of a society inherently commercial, intrinsically intelligent when they can bring their intelligences to bear on practical and concrete propositions, are in their element. The cards are in their hands before their eyes, the stakes are in their pockets, the rules are in their heads. It is a game of quick thinking, not of deep thought. It is an appropriate expression of their instincts and their training. They bend to their bridge as earnestly as anything they undertake in life—an unworthy object for such earnestness? What would you? It is the best they have! The object of a passion counts for little, the passion counts for everything. A great love, whether lavished on a baby or a doll, is an ennobling emotion: a vindictive hatred, whether vented on a husband or a mosquito, is a harmful emotion. So, then, if bridge is played for genuine interest, if bridge lifts its players out of the phantasmagoric aims and interests of their Society into the genuine, the actual, the human, even if these virtues manifest themselves in commercialism mitigated by gambling, nevertheless is bridge an influence to be blessed.

So the night runs on: Society is held together by the centripetal force of clowns, on the one hand, and competitive acquisitiveness, on the other. When, after a few hours more, both of these have served their purpose and preserved to the evening's entertainment its promised halo of success, the guests file past the hostess, appreciating with courteous monotony the hours of delight she has vouchsafed them.

They stream down the monumental stairs and quickly don their coats and wraps. The footman at the door calls their grooms, their chauffeurs, or their coachmen, and as the vehicles draw up their owners walk carelessly out of the artificial radiance of the threshold into the natural blackness of the night. But some few who have suffered from the brilliant obscurity within sigh their relief at the re-enlightenment that awaits them in the darkness.

II

THE OPERA

AS the dinner sees Society at its best, so the opera shows it in its most unfavorable aspect. This is because its object in attending the opera is superlatively artificial.

Men and women and Society alike go to dinners primarily to eat and drink. This is natural: it is what the original dinner was prepared for, centuries before dinners were cooked.

Women and men and (to a considerable extent) Society alike go to balls primarily to dance. This is normal: it is what the original "ball" was devised for, centuries before the most primitive step was systematized.

Men and women go to the opera to enjoy listening to the music. This is fitting: it is what the original tom-tom was beaten for, centuries before one note was known from another. But where these men and women enjoy the music, Society in the main can only endure it. For as a whole its musical sense is quite atrophied.

This being the case, if a set of men and women attended dinners with regularity and relish, having their palates saturated with cocaine, if a hospital of paralytics maintained and patronized a series of weekly hops, their actions would be no more abnormal than those of Society, should it hear music at the opera.

Yet Society does hear music at the opera on Monday night as methodically

NEW YORK SOCIETY ON PARADE

as it says prayers at church on Sunday morning, as religiously as it cuts coupons at the safe deposit on Tuesday afternoon.

The opera begins, socially, at between quarter-past and half-past nine o'clock. At eight o'clock the ordinary audience has begun to pour into the galleries, the upper boxes, and the orchestra seats. At half-past eight the orchestra has started work with an overture, and the proletariat has proved what a curious creature it is by taking this preliminary tuning-up quite seriously and applauding it enthusiastically. A moment later the curtain has risen, and chorus and singers have joined their activities to that of the orchestra. Several of the grand-tier boxes, which are occupied by cultivated people who are only incidentally members of "Society," now gradually fill with silent listeners. After the music has dragged on for three-quarters of an hour or so, the proper atmosphere is attained, the audience is presumably worked up to the proper pitch of anticipation, the *mise en scene* is complete.

There is a stir and rustle behind the velvet curtain at the back of one of the notable grand-tier boxes.

The curtain rattles aside, down to the front of the box sweeps a radiance of satin, a scintillation of diamonds, a lustre of pearls, a glow of rubies, a wanness of skin, a palpitation of fat: Society has reached the opera.

In the front of each box sit either two or three ladies; behind them are either three or four men—each box party consists, therefore, of from five to seven persons. No unsophisticated spectator, surveying such a party, sitting together in ceremonious ease, would guess what a triumph of artifice each natural grouping represents.

What, then, since love of music is negligible, are the rules of composition which the average hostess follows in making up her box party? It is impossible to give a satisfactory answer; the formula is a secret one. All that we definitely know is that the hostess invites her guests because she wishes to extend them the compliment of sharing her box; that her guests accept because they wish to enjoy this compliment. Yet sharing her box is a compliment only because other hostesses have asked other guests for the same reason, and for the same reason other guests have accepted. The box parties go because the opera is fashionable; the opera is fashionable because the box parties go. Which is the cause, and which the effect? Which came first, the egg or the goose?

But the answer seems very much clearer to a philosopher theorizing irresponsibly up in the "peanut gallery." Why, if Society is bored by the music, if Society has all the opportunities for scrutinizing its clothes, its jewels, and its members in the closer proximity of its dinners and its balls, why does Society patronize the opera? Why, replies our philosopher, because exclusive Society, to have any reason for existence, must exclude. It must prove that it is select by showing itself in the midst of those whom it is rejecting. If it lived perpetually in a complete and splendid isolation, the lower classes would have no ocular proof that they were being excluded, while Society itself would have no collective sense of excluding them.

NEW YORK SOCIETY ON PARADE

The opera gives Society a point of contact, and thus of contrast with that horde against whose incursions it is its mission to defend itself. Society's reunion in the visible midst of its foes gives it an *esprit de corps*, a solidarity, which it could never secure or maintain by uninterrupted aloofness. If it were not for the many who are called, the few who are chosen would not experience any peculiar gratification. Thus Society instinctively feels that its presence at the opera is indispensable both to tantalize the vulgar into more poignant envy, and to tone up its own morale for more zealous self-defence —or so thinks our somewhat socialistic friend in the "peanut gallery."

Whatever the motive may be, the hostess does graciously invite her guests, and the guests do avidly accept her invitation. They are generally asked to a

NEW YORK SOCIETY ON PARADE

preliminary dinner, which is, as a rule, pushed forward to half-past seven o'clock so that they may reach the opera before the close of the first act. This is desirable so that the disturbance of their entrance, their removal of coats and wraps, their respective allotment of seats by the hostess, may take place while the music is still going on, and may not interrupt the social exercises of the *entr'acte*. There are, however, a few illustrious exceptions to this custom, who, being above such convention, do not vouchsafe their entrance until the height of the first *entr'acte*, holding themselves in reserve so that their final advent may, in the eyes of all, remove suspense as to their whereabouts and cap the climax of the opera's brilliance.

At some date between their acceptance of the invitations and the appointed night most of the guests glance at the advertisements in their papers to ascertain, not the composer who is to be interpreted, not the opera which is to be rendered, but the singers who are to officiate. If they find that these singers are the most celebrated artists, who command the highest salaries, they feel gratified. If the singers are ones who have not yet earned such reputation or extorted such salaries, they are disappointed. They are not in the least interested to assist at the experimental début of a new artist (unless perhaps the singer has brought over a Continental reputation for beauty and notoriety for frailty); they are not in the least excited by the possibility of hearing the beauties of an unknown voice make it famous in a few hours of song. They prefer song which is so expensive that it must be the best. They prefer to trust to the impresario's purse rather than to their own ears as the criterion of art.

However, gratified or disappointed on this minor point, they make their appearance at their hostess's house at half-past seven, and settle themselves to their dinner with amiable appreciation, oblivious to the fact that as the *entrée* is served the orchestra must be tuning up, as the meat is passed the overture must be swelling through the house, as the bird is tasted the curtain must be rising on the first act.

The dinner being leisurely completed, the hostess remarks dubiously to her husband that she supposes the men might perhaps smoke their cigars on the way to the opera. This is probably more from a kindly desire to free the women from one another's society in the drawing-room than from any desire to reach the opera earlier, but the men always acquiesce, and climb into one carriage or automobile with their cigars and cigarettes while the ladies enjoy one another's company in another vehicle.

On reaching the opera they walk up one flight of stairs, to the distant muffled murmurs of the orchestra and an occasional high note from one of the singers, loud enough to force its way out to them. These solitary and sudden notes, robbed of all musical quality by the inaudibility of their context, sound as if some sublimated butcher-shop within were being operated to slow music. But one of the guests, at some unusually penetrating scream, is sure to breathe "Ah!" (as she hastens her steps up the stairs); "Ah!" in tones of tender and preposterous appreciation. Why she does it she could not herself explain, for she has not the least intention of listening to the music when she reaches the box. It is probably done from the same instinct that would make her honestly declare, if questioned, that she was devoted to music or to children, although she might not know a fugue in one from a whooping-cough out of the other. A curious traditional attribute of her sex, this devotion to music and children, which she still feels it seemly to subscribe to in theory.

When the party reaches the top of the stairs a liveried usher shows them to the door of their box, which he unlocks and opens for them. On this door is a plate bearing the name of their host if he is enviable enough to own the box, or of some one else if he is merely rich enough to rent it. There is a certain subtle difference of emotion, which almost every opera guest has experienced, between sitting in an owned and in a hired box. In the rented box the guest feels the privilege of presence, but in the owned box she feels the prestige of possession, feels with a twinge of veneration that her hosts actually own the number of square feet of music that enter their box, actually own that proportion of tenor, soprano, and baritone; of brass and strings and wood-wind; of the passion and beauty and boredom of the musical opera; of the fashion and brilliance and fascination of the social opera—it is the difference between having the admirable portrait of an unknown man shown by a public guide, on a museum wall, and having an old master's portrait of an illustrious ancestor pointed out by his distinguished descendant, on his dining-room wall. It is the difference between the expensive bottle of wine your host buys for you at a restaurant and the precious bottle which he brings up for you from his family cellar. It is all the added value of tradition and association that casts its glamour of mellow vanity on the box party whose host's name is on the box door.

The usher having unlocked the door, a neat maid hastens up to help the ladies off with their opera cloaks and their fur overshoes. The little room at the back of the box becomes for a few moments a scene of bewildering confusion before Nature is extricated from her shrouds, a powdered medley of writhing arms, contorted backs, twisted necks, and heaving bosoms. One or two of the men generally add to the confusion by helping the ladies off with their things, while the other men stand in the hall pulling on and buttoning their white gloves, until finally all the superfluous clothes are hanging on the walls and lying across the sofa and the chairs. Then the men follow into the small room and dispose of their own hats and coats in any odd corners of the floor that may remain available.

It is then that the hostess, pulling aside the curtain with a rattle which the music almost drowns, sweeps down to the front of the box and indicates to the other ladies which of the front seats they are to adorn. The men are ranged behind the women by chance, by choice, or by adversity, the whole party settles itself in comfort with a few delicate wriggles, and, raising its battery of opera-glasses, throws itself into the duty and the pleasure of the occasion. The other boxes are by this time filled or filling. The "Horse-shoe" presents engrossing interest; it is a kaleidoscopic combination of clothes and jewels and women and men, to be analyzed and criticised to the spleen's content. Many boxes are of course comparatively uninteresting. The women in them have to be dismissed as looking worse, or, occasionally, better than usual. But, then, in other boxes may be discovered the pathos of a woman wearing the very same dress she wore to the opera a week ago; the problem of a woman of moderate means wearing a string of pearls which must be either adulterated or adulterous; the romance of a young couple who were blessed with their first baby only a fortnight before; the tragedy of the noble earl, imported by one fond mother, sitting in another mother's box; the satire of the social climber who has at last mysteriously managed to get herself into the Society leader's box; the comedy of the senti- mental - looking couple just back from their wedding trip, with the bride's lately divorced husband sitting at her elbow in the next box. These are only the obvious features that the first sweep of the opera-glasses brings into view. Imagine, then, what interesting revelations, what tantalizing mysteries, what thrilling certainties, will yield themselves to the patient and minute investigation which is to follow.

Our hostess, after the first preliminary sweep of her opera-glasses, postpones the more delicate scrutiny and leans back to enjoy a moment's passive satisfaction. For she has already seen enough to know that her party, in membership and adornment, has no superior among the other boxes. Has she not, sitting next her, the beautiful Englishwoman whose ambitious indiscretions are admitted to be regal in their field of operation, who is spending a few weeks in New York, and who is most fastidious in her acceptance of invitations? Has she not placed next to this quasi-royal guest her own lovely stepdaughter by her husband's divorced wife, an act of maternal solicitude which she could not have improved on if the girl had been her own daughter by her divorced husband? Is not her English guest a dazzling marvel in dress and jewels? Is not her lovely stepdaughter a shimmering triumph of extravagant simplicity—her dress, her dog-collar, her demeanor all virginally quiet, obviously most expensive? Is not her own appearance the most incomparably splendid which taste and money can provide?

She is proud of the appearance of her box, she is delighted at the appearance of the other women. For the opera has lifted her to such dizzy heights of artificiality that she has left the woman far below and is now but the disembodied hostess. She does not resent the splendor of the women next her, she does not wish to eclipse them, she does not fear their eclipsing her, she is perfectly willing, if need be, to shine in reflected jewels. All for which she yearns is that they will collaborate with her to make her box the most brilliant at the opera.

As for the men: there is the husband of the Englishwoman who has been accepted with his wife, although society has been rather shocked at the open way, under the circumstances, in which they travel together. Next him sits the most eligible young man in New York, of very good family, very rich, very well behaved; who was at first considered stupid, but who has vindicated himself by learning to drive a four in masterly fashion. He is afraid that he will be married by her stepdaughter, but has accepted her invitation, notwithstanding. Behind the Englishman sits the clever architect who writes such cynical articles about society, and goes about only in its most exclusive set. He makes short remarks which she does not understand, but which, she is informed, are called epigrams and are intellectual. At any rate, his presence shows that she can command literary as well as social eminence. Next to him, in the remote back of the box, sits her husband, smiling benignly, she feels sure. He always smiles like that when he is thinking of a new railroad he plans to add to his collection. She wishes he would not think of business at the opera. She has often told him what a Philistine proceeding it is. But, after all, he is the most prominent figure in the financial

THE "HORSE-SHOE" AT ITS BEST

world of his day, so his presence in her party rounds out its eclectic selectness. At this moment the box party becomes vaguely aware that something has just happened, and, on shaking itself free from its reveries and descending to material things, it finds that the music has suddenly stopped, that the curtain has just fallen on the first act, and that a large portion of the audience are on their feet applauding with violence.

The light blazes more brilliantly throughout the auditorium, no longer subordinated to the footlights and the calcium; the ordinary audience breaks from silence into conversation, and society in the boxes continues its conversations in freer tones, no longer trammelled by the orchestra and singers.

The "Horse-shoe" is now seen at what it would consider its best. A curious "best" it is. The stark illumination undoubtedly brings out every shade of silk, satin, and velvet. It beats on every facet of every jewel to the most perfect advantage. Perhaps it beguiles the flowers dying on the women's breasts into feeling themselves back beneath the sunrise. But when it touches the flesh and blood of the women themselves it changes its tactics. It used to suck all the color from their faces and spread over them instead a harsh and haggard tinge. It used to pounce on foibles with the ingenuity of a caricaturist and nurse them into blatent blemishes, deepening the slight shadows of thinness into the dark hollows of emaciation, strengthening the high-lights of plumpness into the swollen shininess of obesity.

This mocking mischief of the chiaroscuro has been corrected by a chivalrous management, but the remedy has grave defects of its own. For the light, bullied out of its former vagaries, now casts itself on its victims in a non-committal, stolid glare which reduces them one and all to utter uniformity and indescribable inanity. There are no laughably fat women, no pitifully thin women, no sheepish women, no waspish women, no bovine women, no feline women—no women. For the light refuses to accord to beauty the truth that it withholds from ugliness. If it is forced to ignore human imperfections it will assuredly not emphasize feminine perfections. If it is not permitted to indulge itself in personalities, neither will it indulge its victims in individualities. So there they sit, side by side, in their scores and in their hundreds, women in reality beautiful or ugly, clever or stupid, refined or coarse-grained, pure or sensual, modest or bold, sweet or hard: to be loved, to be won, to be cherished, to be slaved for; to be gulled, to be betrayed, to be abused, to be forgotten—enough women in potentiality to redeem or to annihilate the world.

There they sit, side by side, in their scores and in their hundreds, women who are in semblance wax dolls one and all, mere supports for their dresses, mere backgrounds for their jewels, mere mannikins worked by a cynical ventriloquist to grin and gesture with automatic animation, to pose and preen with pomp and dignity; all cast in one mould, and, God help us, the mould not cracked in the casting.

And the pitiful part of it is that the light is all the while rendering a sardonic obedience to their desires, fashioning itself into a sneering angel of truth. It

A YOUNG MAN OF EXCELLENT FAMILY BUT
NO FORTUNE, AND—OF NO PROSPECTS

emphasizes what they cherish, it discounts what they neglect. If it caresses tenderly every fold of drapery, every subtlest tint and texture of moiré and brocade, if it dallies passionately with every depth and shallow of every gem, if it obliterates every reflection of mind and heart, every expression of soul and understanding, what is it doing that they are not doing? If they prefer to be admired for their clothes rather than for their qualities, for their mineral appendages rather than for their moral attributes, is the light not ministering to their predilections?

Hardly has the curtain fallen on the first act when the door of our opera party's box clicks open and a young man enters and pays his respects to the ladies. He is a young man of excellent family but of no fortune, and (as he has wilfully become a dramatic critic instead of a broker's clerk) of no prospects. He is deeply in love with the hostess's stepdaughter; she finds him a curious and alluring novelty, for he has a profusion of ideas, which he exposes quite indecently to the point of view of one who, like her, has been educated to believe that the larger portions of the brain as well as of the body are not supposed to exist in polite society. At his entrance the most eligible young man in New York and the Englishman take the opportunity of departing to pay some visits of their own. The hostess considers the new-comer to be a young man of cleverness, and therefore presumably of bad form. She regards him with deep suspicion, and therefore engages him in animated conversation, to his distress and her stepdaughter's annoyance. She knows he is the type of person who is probably interested in the goings-on beyond the footlights, and so tactfully turns the conversation to operatic art by asking him whether he does not think that the soprano has kept her figure wonderfully for her age, while the contralto must have gained fully twenty pounds since last season, and the tenor does look absurd without his own mustache.

The door clicks open again and a middle-aged man mouses in to speak to the English celebrity. He has been an intimate friend of hers in London in the days of her virtuous obscurity, and wonders whether she will remember him again. As he seats himself the hostess's husband disappears. The Englishwoman asks her old friend if he does not consider it shocking that such an opera as the one given last Monday should be permitted on the stage in New York to corrupt public morals—she is happy to say that it has never got by the censor in England.

The door swings open again, and in comes an elderly young man of twenty-five or thereabouts. He considers himself under social obligations to the hostess for past hospitalities and future entertainments, and is expected to attach himself in public to his fashionable patroness, just as the plebeian clients of Augustan Rome found it incumbent to follow in the train of their aristocratic patrons in their walks through streets and forum. He suavely but surely usurps the conversation with the hostess, leaving the dramatic critic the pleasant task of stepping into the shoes of the departing architect by entertaining the stepdaughter. This is precisely what the hostess wishes to avoid, but with well-trained self-control she conceals her vexation by remarking to the elderly young man that she sees his grandmother is wearing her Pearls tonight. He professes surprise, as he had understood the Pearls were being cleaned at the jeweller's, and had therefore taken for granted that she would wear the Sapphires. They then remark with interest which of their jewels several other women are wearing. For hostesses and their social clients (at the opera, at least) are very much more familiar with their friends' gems than with their children, and take a deep and affectionate interest in their families of precious stones, from their first-born necklace to the new-born stomacher which is the joy and consolation of their age.

And now, just at the moment when, all through the glittering "Horse-shoe," young ineligibles are creeping closest to their ladies' hearts, old friends are becoming most dubious as to one another's loss of reputations, young protégées are shedding most lustre upon their social suzerains—just as the opera is reaching its climacteric—the lights go out, the orchestra begins to bang and clash, and Society has to plunge into the dismal anticlimax of the music and song, with nothing to mitigate it but patiently subdued conversation. After the first few bars of music the male inhabitants of the box come slinking in, like beasts of prey returning to their lair, and the visitors have to return to their own respective parties.

The second act necessitating, for some absurd theatrical reason, a darkened auditorium, the well-bred patience of Society deserves a world of credit. Do they pay very large prices for their boxes, and expend much time and trouble on their personal appearance, merely to crouch whispering in the dark, like silly children at a magic-lantern show? And yet not a moan of protest, scarcely a sigh of complaint, escapes them. They sit murmuring affably in one another's ears, with their eyes fixed vacantly on the relative brightness of the stage, paying a sort of automatic heed to the gesticulations and vociferations of the excited little men and women down beyond the footlights, occasionally remarking with gentle pity the absurd contortions of the poor crazed conductor. One of the women seems to be waving a veil from the steps of an old castle; two men come into the dim garden below; one woman and one man go away; the other woman and the other man begin singing to each other, sitting on a bench in the dim garden, locked in each other's arms. The woman is the soprano who has kept her figure so remarkably; she has one of the very largest salaries in the world, and necessarily one of the very finest voices. The man is the tenor who has shaved off his mustache. His voice and his salary are as superlative as hers. As they go on singing a good many of the boxes become strangely hushed, many of the vacant gazes grow attentive. For this is wonderful singing, and, strange as it may seem, a large proportion of Society can appreciate wonderful singing. Through attending the opera at least once a week steadily, opera season after opera season, through being compelled to hear, at its musicales, nothing but the picked voices of the world, Society has undergone a subconscious education, has suffered cultivation despite itself. It still knows nothing whatsoever of orchestral music, it still cares nothing whatsoever for vocal music as music, for it still feels nothing whatsoever of the beauties of a splendid voice. But it does find an intelligent satisfaction in hearing a voice as competently employed as possible. It knows and disapproves immediately when a note is flat or sharp, or veiled or has a tremolo, not because it feels the slightest pain at the ugliness of the note, but because it knows that the voice is not doing its work perfectly, and it wants its voices, like its automobiles or its stock-tickers, to run accurately and without hitch.

So most of the boxes listen attentively to the singing, and, though none of its beauty penetrates to their emotions, yet somehow, taken with the acting and the setting, they realize that the most passionate of love-scenes is being sung and suffered in their presence. And as it is the fat and sodden men who find the keenest enjoyment in watching the physical endurance of a prize-fight, so these flat-chested girls and anæmic women find a pleasurable filip to their imaginations in the molten passion of this love duet.

But the lovers are interrupted by a reproachful basso with an interminable song, and the boxes return to their muttered conversations. The auditorium becomes somewhat lighter, and Society forgets the stage and the throbbing music, and engages itself once more in inspecting and in being inspected.

Now can be witnessed to the best advantage the functioning of a curious sixth sense possessed by Society, one all its own—the sense of exhibition. Although this sense cannot be analyzed, it is as indubitable as that of direction in carrier-pigeons. If Society at the opera were blindfolded so that it could see no admiring glances, had its ears stuffed so that it could hear no adulatory applause, had its nostrils stopped so that it could smell no incense, and had its powers of touch and taste for the time being suspended also, to be on the safe side, nevertheless it would still sense the presence of observation, and would preen itself as spontaneously as it would make a wry face at a bitter taste, or flinch at a violent sound, or start at a pin-prick.

Amid the pleasures and the profits of this mutual observation the rest of the act elapses, unnoticed and unresented. The curtain falls upon the stage and rises upon the second *entr'acte* amid the thunderous applause of a seemingly hysterical populace. The hostess, her stepdaughter, and her English guest have now apparently observed all there is worth notice in the other boxes and know all that should be known of their occupants. The desire to see has been satiated, the desire to be seen alone survives. But, as all the other ladies in all the other boxes share these sentiments with one accord, the business of the evening threatens to come to a standstill. Now it is that the eyes of the party wander listlessly from the other boxes down to the orchestra seats. There they note what will always be a puzzle to such eyes. For scattered among these seats are the familiar faces of many acquaintances and friends, all fellow-members of Society. Some of them could easily afford opera boxes of their own, many of them could have accepted invitations to other people's opera boxes. Yet they prefer to sit huddled in promiscuous rows, and seem all the while to be instinct with enjoyment. These are the men and women of Society who come to-night from sheer desire for music, to let the world in which they work and worry drift from their sight, and for a little while live in that land of visions to which the thrill and thraldom of the music alone can lift them. They are Society's minority of sane, straight men and women, too few to stamp their soundness on its spuriousness, but none the less a vivifying few who prove in Society's behalf that breeding is compatible with brains, polite associations with intelligent interests, and all the pomp of polished worldliness with the homely virtues of decent citizens.

As the second *entr'acte* ends and the curtain rises on the last act our party is by now reduced to straits of monotony. They are tired of looking at their friends, which is regrettable. Their friends are tired of looking at them, which is intolerable. They are tired of talking to one another, which is natural. They have no resource left but self-communion, and that is tantamount to excommunication. At length, as a last desperate resort, the hostess fixes her veiled attention on the box next her on the left. Its owner has been driven, among the other privations of a panic, to rent this box for alternate Monday nights to a family of rank outsiders, a piece of treachery to his caste which even his dilemma leaves it difficult to forgive. In the box sit these people whom our hostess does not know. True, her husband is acquainted with the man during business hours down in Wall Street; true, she herself has met the woman, his wife, at a benefit which she was once misguided enough to attend as patroness; true, her stepdaughter has been at school with the daughter of this couple. But she assuredly does not know them, and between the inmates of the two boxes, sitting a few inches apart, rises a film of ice, transparent but frigidly impassable. Now, through this film our hostess warily watches her neighbors. She feels astonished resentment at the way in which these persons manage to ape the appearance and the manners of their betters. The woman's dress is perfection, not high enough or quiet enough to seem *bourgeois*, not too low or too vulgar to be fashionable. Her jewels, too, sound just the proper note of ostentation. Her face strikes a nice balance between artifice and nature. Her voice is perhaps too well modulated to be in the best of form, but she undoubtedly has the effrontery to wear an air of natural distinction. Her husband is a fine-looking, well-mannered man, her daughter a little thing apparently of grace and of refinement. Our hostess heaves a sigh. She realizes that these strangers are her subtlest foes, who weaken Society by sapping the rigor of its exclusiveness. To-day they are not known, to-morrow they are already within the gates, the next day who knows but they may be the self-appointed guardians of Society's most sacred shrines. She understands that a little judiciously selected new blood adds strength to her order, but let in too much new blood, destroy the nice balance between the multitude of eager aspirants to her rank and the few selected for the privilege of promotion, and dimly she feels that no one will prize what every one can have, and that Society will go down to extinction in a convulsion of exploded self-esteem.

Finally as even such forebodings fail any longer to hold her attention, the music forces itself more and more remorselessly upon her and her companions. They find their ears being morbidly drawn to it, just as their eyes might be drawn again and again to some horrible sight they did not wish to see. They cannot escape the delirious ravings of the wounded hero. They do not know that his yearnings are for his mistress's ship; they do know that theirs are for their hostess's automobile. Were they but gifted with his vocal chords, they might sing their impatience as earnestly as he. They have no faithful henchman to soothe their fevered brows and comfort their distress. They cannot even, as a last resort, end the suspense by tearing bandages from bleeding wounds.

They must sit, and sit, in stoic resignation. For if they left as yet they would arrive too early at the dance for which they are bound. And so, their bracelets growing into manacles, their necklaces into cold, heavy fetters, their rings into hard thumb-screws, their tiaras into slow-shrinking iron torture-caps, they gallantly set their teeth, and, with never a writhe or whimper of their suffering, sit on in their vast and brilliant torture-chamber, heroic slaves to duty and decorum.

But now at last after a murmured consultation the hostess rises, the rest following her example. As they stand there for a moment their weary eyes wander for the glad last time to the stage from which they are escaping. There the hero has apparently just died, and the heroine, kneeling beside his body, is just beginning to sing.

The curtain of the box rattles back, and the party, chatting briskly, passes out into the little room behind. They agree that they are leaving at exactly the right moment. By taking their time in getting into their wraps, and counting on the usual delay in getting their automobile, they will reach the dance at just about the proper time.

Meanwhile many other curtains rattle open, letting rays of light flash merrily across the auditorium as the box parties pass cheerily out on their way to the dance or to their homes. The boxes of the "Horse-shoe" become, with some exceptions, suddenly deserted.

The opera is over. All that is left is the ordinary audience, sitting with throbbing hearts and misty eyes and choking throats, pierced by the music of the *Liebestodt*.

III

THE DANCE

AT the dinner we have seen Society saved from itself literally by the skin of its teeth. At the opera it could not save itself by the skin of its neck. What will be its deportment at a dance?

Of all forms of social entertainment the dance has always been most inseparably identified with spontaneous gayety.

Mankind still uses the ceremony of eating to celebrate its grief as well as its happiness, sorrowfully gorging on funeral bake-meats as readily as it joyfully battens on wedding-cake. It has always similarly used the art of music, weeping to a death dirge as naturally as it laughs at a music-hall ditty.

But, from the fierce exultation of the Indians leaping round the torture-stake to the solemn exaltation of the dancing choir-boys of Seville pacing their measures on the steps of the High Altar, from the jocularity of the jig to the stately pleasure of the minuet, man has reserved the dance as the appropriate expression of his elation.

Can men and women, however denatured their instincts, so emasculate the spirit of the dance that, locked in each other's arms, swinging through the gay radiance of the ball-room to the compelling rhythm of the music, the poetry of motion may become to them nothing but the prose of exertion, their partners be to their utter indifference nothing but necessary stage properties for the parts that they are playing, their hearts be filled only with the sordid satisfaction of gratified rapacity, their minds be filled only with the selfish schemes of social exploitation?

These are the questions which the ball must answer for itself.

The hostess issues the invitations to her dance only a week or even five days before the event. At first thought this might seem to be a mistake, giving a suggestion of the impromptu with its attendant geniality and informality, to what should be an august and deliberate ceremonial. But deeper consideration will show that this very briefness of notice is a circumstance full of pomp and prestige. It demonstrates that the hostess is a lady of such calibre that she need fear the rival entertainments of no lesser ladies on the evening of her choice; that her invitations are paramount, to be eagerly accepted, no matter what else her guests had planned for that night. The only danger in this method—that one of the few other hostesses of equal position with herself should chance to choose the same night for a ball of her own—is avoided by each of these hostesses having secured the social rights to a certain week in winter for her annual ball, and on this week none of her equals would think of infringing.

The invitations inform the hostess's prospective guests that she will be "At Home" at half-past ten of a certain night. In the lower left-hand corner of the card the single word "cotillion" indicates the reason for her domesticity.

Commonplace-looking enough, these little pieces of pasteboard, and accepted as such by most of those who receive them. But there are some to whom they are of pitifully vital moment, some whose fingers tremble as they tear open the envelope to make sure that it is this very invitation which is inside, some who, having found their hopes realized, gloat over the little piece of pasteboard as though it were a love-letter or a divorce decree, feel that their years of Sysiphus-labor, pushing their precious stones up the heights of social prominence, have reached their successful end at last, feel that this little card is their letter-patent of nobility, feel that in a moment they have become finer and loftier men and women, worthier to take their places next to those exalted personages whom they have so long envied and revered from afar. Thus can this little card unloose all that mighty passion which may be entitled

NEW YORK SOCIETY ON PARADE

hero-worship or called snobbishness, as an invitation is received or not.

The night of nights has come. The lower classes of New York, from their Hester Street tenements to their Riverside Drive mansions, are profoundly unperturbed. They go through their routine, dining or starving, wining or worrying, costuming or freezing, sinning or snoring, without a thought of the ball that is to be. In all these lower classes the only interested parties are the hostess's servants; the caterers; the decorators; the guests' maids, their coachmen, footmen, and chauffeurs; some wives of millionaires who, when they tore open the envelopes with trembling fingers, found that the card inside was not *the* card; the orchestras; some Society reporters; and a couple of detectives. But though New York as a city is unmoved, New York as a Society is stirred to whatever depths it can command. Such functions as to-night's are not only the objects but the mainstays of its existence. Its members in their line of carriages and motors, leading up to the hostess's door, will sit, as much dependent for their social sustenance on what she will provide as the kindred line down on the Bowery depends on its dole of bread.

In scores of the palatial plagiarisms which make Fifth Avenue the architectural museum of the world, the dining-rooms are filled with unusual animation at the prospect of the imminent event. It is the first big ball of the season, the first pitched battle of the campaign, the first opportunity for each to see exactly where he or she stands; to note the subtle promotions and degradations which take place from year to year; to miss the familiar faces of those on whom Death has paid his party call; to observe the unfamiliar faces of those who have been knocking at the social door so long, who have just been admitted, but who have not yet been relieved of their hats and wraps; to study the fresh blood—the band of this year's débutantes, the bevy of college graduates.

In a hundred humbler homes French maids are spreading out their mistresses' finery, while these examine their deadly armory as a duellist tests the temper of his rapier, or the hair-trigger of his pistol, before starting for the field of honor. Especially, in each house that guards the treasure of a débutante, is excitement at the snapping-point. Mother, maid, butler, father—all breathlessly run errands and send messages on behalf of their young mistress, who, pale but grim, nods impatiently at the last words of maternal advice, thanks the butler graciously for having hurried up the automobile, and snaps at the paternal clumsiness which has almost placed a foot upon her train.

The home of the ball is of course the centre of suspense. The hostess herself is unruffled. She is a proud and worldly wise lady who has been giving her balls year before year as far back as she cares to remember. With her wealth and her position the giving of a ball reduces itself to a very simple formula. She has quickly edited her last year's list of guests up to date, adding here, erasing there, as deaths, débuts, and divorces necessitate, and has with judicial discrimination elevated a few worthy outsiders to the ranks of Society. She has then instructed her secretary to address invitations to the names on her list. Having selected the young man whom she wishes to lead her cotillion, she has then ordered the flowers, the food, the orchestras, and the favors as methodically as she has ordered the guests. It never occurs to her to speculate as to whether her guests will fail to enjoy themselves any more than as to whether any of them may fall and break their legs. Such worries she leaves to the majority of hostesses who have to give balls for a social livelihood. As for herself, it is not a question whether her ball will seem a success to her guests, but whether her guests will be a success at her ball. It may as well be confessed at once that she is not typical of most hostesses of New York Society, but she is typical of what they would all like to be, and this is an occasion on which it seems more magnanimous to typify the few ideals than the many actualities.

So the hostess sits quite placidly reading a French novel, while the "beauty doctor," whom she has imported from Paris and has made the fashion in New York, kneads her face and neck with grease, whose magic properties assure a perpetual middle age. But while she is discarding wrinkles, her housekeeper and her butler are acquiring them, worrying over all the final details of preparation. Such is the responsibility of the moment, that they have buried their chronic feud and are cordially co-operating for the honor of the house. Their trials are multifarious indeed. Their most decorative footman has found the thought of all the champagne which is to be consumed this night too much for his sympathetic soul, and has fallen a hopeless victim to premature intoxication. A certain patch on the ball-room floor refuses to wax properly, and remains a Slough of Despond in the midst of its slippery environment. The S. P. C. A. has sent an official to announce that if one of the cotillion figures consists of the ladies offering live guinea-pigs, as favors, to snakes held by the gentlemen (as prognosticated in the *Evening Screamer,* with the snarling sycophancy of its kind), their society will have to stop the brutal proceeding. The word of honor of the butler and a pint of champagne are needed to assuage this gentleman's humanitarian fears. There is a deadlock as to who is to serve the coffee and sandwiches to the coachmen and chauffeurs, which requires diplomatic handling. The detectives show gallantry to the upper housemaid and the second parlor-maid, instantly causing intricate domestic complications. But of these sordid details, and many more like them, the hostess knows nothing, as, with rejuvenated face, she passes from the hands of the French sorceress to those of the coiffeur.

The house is now ready for the fray. It beams and glitters with pride and satisfaction. At last, for a few brief hours, it will be in its element, it will be allowed to perform its proper functions, to fulfil those purposes for which it was designed five hundred years ago in the flood-tide of the Renaissance: to hold the crowded courts of princes; to frame the gorgeous pageantry of worldly power; to glow as background to its glory; to guard the secrets of its infamies; to throb with the unceasing rush of many lives, elbowing one another through its busy halls; to shelter and to know them in their pomp and in their nakedness; to echo with the sighs of love and of satiety; to silently suck up the blood of stabbings and the froth of poisonings; but always to be full of life, rich, vivid, manifold.

Poor house, designed for such a destiny, what a lonely, empty anticlimax is its fate. Its big proportions, its large perspectives, its stately heights and monumental spaces, which would have stretched in harmonious welcome to thronging vassals, courtiers, functionaries, here frown in cold, forbidding vastness upon the void existence which they contain. An elderly lady, her son living abroad, her daughter married, holds her solitary court within its walls, with a nursery of lap-dogs and a negligible husband who spends the days of a dummy director and the nights of a dummy debauché. A well-ordered lady whose life is one of dulness and of dignity; a remote lady who welcomes few visitors and no emotions

NEW YORK SOCIETY ON PARADE

into her daily life; a lady of power as absolute in its way as that of any despot whom the house in its own day might have held, but who never lets the picturesque or the spectacular impinge upon her sway, preferring the silent, certain unobtrusiveness of twentieth-century power. Day after day the house yawns cavernously, an empty setting for an empty life, while two streams, of tradesmen and of trucklers, leave packages and visiting-cards at its servants' entrance and its front door, and only a few friends are privileged to patter through its echoing emptinesses, to lunch or dine with its mistress in the comparative comfort of her breakfast-room.

But to-night the house has roused itself from its torpor. To-night it will feast on life, gorge itself with humanity. To-night it will throb with thronging flesh

NEW YORK SOCIETY ON PARADE

and blood, thrill with passions hot from the hearts of many men and women, stir with plans and plottings cold from their brains. To-night the house will once more come into its own—or so it thinks.

The time has come. The invitations have been issued for half-past ten. It is half-past eleven. Two rows of footmen in plush knee-breeches stretch from the entrance across the marble wastes of hall, and up the desolate sweep of soaring staircase, two slender threads by which the first guests can find their intrepid path up to the hospitable Minotaur who lies in wait above.

At half-past eleven the first covey of guests flits in, finds refuge in the cloakrooms, and stealthily waits for reinforcements. These early arrivals are unfortunates who were not able to get invitations to either of the opera-houses. They have been unable to pass the evening at the theatre because to wear décolleté dresses there would be improper, owing to the obscure law which in our country has until recently made it indecent to expose at the play those identical physical expanses which it is obligatory to exhibit at the opera. They have therefore been doomed to domesticity, and have been dragging themselves through the endless hours since dinner, in the arid atmosphere of home, nervously alternating between the easy-chair, the piano, the bookcase, and the dressing-table. At the earliest possible moment they have shaken the dust of their habitations from their slippers, and, accompanied by mother, brother, husband, or maid, have sped to the ball.

When enough arrivals have gathered

to give one another moral support, they begin their advance. Across the hall they wend their way with stately tread and dignified composure. Then up the majestic stairs the climbing cortège winds, its full-flung trains draping the steps with glory, and, having gained the summit, in glittering array sweeps slowly toward the hostess. In a great doorway, her triumphal arch, flanked by her married daughter, she stands, an imposing figure, instinct with formality and power. The stiff lines of her satin dress, the steady glitter of her diamonds, the rigid coiffure of her pale hair, the tautened crispness of her skin (the victory of massage over matter), her straight carriage, all show the born leader of women. Her guests file past her with the air of sumptuous gladiators crying dauntlessly: "Hail, Hostess! We who are about to dance salute thee!" She, too, acknowledges their passage with what is more nearly a salute than a greeting.

Having rendered homage, the guests move on into the great ball-room. They stand for a moment in little huddled groups on the outskirts of its vast spaces of polished floor, bathed in its bright light, rocked in the rhythmic waves of music with which the orchestra is flooding the room, from its ambush of ferns and flowers.

This should by rights be a precious moment. Have they not come to dance? Are their feet not caressed by a perfect floor, are their ears not tempted by persuasive music, are their eyes not beckoned to by spaciousness in which they can abandon themselves unhampered to the full harmonious sweep of movement matched to melody? They should speed to each other's arms, and swing away through time and space as exultingly as skylarks soar or eagles swoop—or so thinks a poetic detective, standing in an alcove, keeping an eye on the cotillion favors.

But this does not seem to happen. Some dozen débutantes, with the enthusiasm of their inexperience, thrill with delight at the spectacle of a floor on which there is room to dance, and, with their loyal partners, glide ingenuously to and fro, enjoying themselves prettily. But, for the most part, in more seasoned breasts the sight of the unfilled floor arouses feelings of despondency. They are oppressed by a sense of loneliness in the great room, a sense of disappointment that more people are not already here, a keen expectancy for that moment when the room will be choked with guests and the night will really attain its brilliancy.

Each moment, however, lessens their isolation. For the guests continue to march past the hostess in a continuous stream, and are already making promising inroads on the free floor space of the room.

Surely the hostess has reason to feel satisfaction beneath her impassivity. Her vassals make a very gallant showing as in their silk and satin squadrons they file before her and deploy on the polished field of battle. The girls and women are of a higher average of beauty than any European ball-room could produce. Standing or moving erect, they show their figures and their clothes to better advantage than they could seated at the dinner-table. Thrown together at close quarters, amid the stimulating familiarity of friends and enemies, they present their faces to better advantage than they could posed in the show-case of the opera box. The men, too, are generally well-built, tall, and handsome, easily distinguishable from the waiters. Only the débutantes are, as a whole, disappointing. With childish faces and undeveloped forms, they seem pitifully immature to be proclaimed ready for the responsibilities of life. But they have been carefully coached to a thorough familiarity with their duties to Society, and are, most of them, already precocious women of the world; so, as their responsibilities will be primarily social ones, they are readier to bear them than they seem. As for the subordinate problems of marriage and maternity, these can easily be left to their husbands and their children.

Now the second orchestra, which has

been furnished to alternate with the first so that there shall be no lapses in the music, arouses itself from its dejected attitude of waiting for the worst, and from its end of the room takes up the relay race of melody. It is by this time playing to standing-room only. The great room is filled with a dazzling mass of fashionable humanity. Those who have escaped from the operas have added themselves to those who have escaped from the homes. The crowd stands, its members jostling one another politely, nodding, smiling, shaking hands, turning the cold shoulder, seeing, making itself seen. The dancers have become congested into an amorphous mass which oozes round and round. From time to time this viscous whirlpool casts out an exhausted and bedraggled couple, and from time to time a fresh pair, united in the holy bonds

APPRAISED FOR THE BEAUTY OF THEIR FACES
OR THE BOUNTY OF THEIR FAMILIES

of waltz or two-step, wedge their way into the struggle.

No one can for a moment doubt that the dancers are doing their duty. But in the seemingly aimless conglomeration which covers the rest of the floor, a useful work is also proceeding. The débutantes are being assorted and appraised, for the beauty of their faces or the bounty of their families. Men, attracted for the one or the other reason, secure introductions, chat a moment, and then cement the new acquaintance by a plunge into the turmoil of the dance. When a girl has neither the features nor the fortune to lure men to her as willing devotees, they are nevertheless led up as vicarious victims by her mother, her chaperon, her brother, their friends. These victims also increase by a sort of compound interest, for, to liberate themselves, they frequently do not hesitate to betray a friend. Thus the poor girl frequently meets as many men in her first *mauvais quart d'heure* as do her luckier sisters, passing from hand to hand with an alacrity that pathetically simulates popularity, until she may chance to encounter some eccentric fellow who, even at a ball, sets store on cultivated tastes or an educated mind; who, perhaps, finds in her these morbid propensities, and settles with her into satisfied companionship.

All over the room other men are busily engaged in asking women to be their partners for supper or cotillion, or as busily engaged in avoiding asking them. The women, on their side, graciously accept these proposals when they come from desirable parties. When, however, they come from men with whom a dance might be regarded as a mesalliance, diplomacy frequently becomes the order of the night, each lady suspending her would-be partner in that state of benign and befuddled uncertainty which woman alone has the skill to induce, and man alone the simplicity to endure, while she awaits further applications. Accordingly, as a more congenial partner presents himself or not, her original supplicant is then daintily discarded or duly utilized. It is interesting to observe, in this manœuvre, how closely the lady follows the matrimonial method. Indeed, it is one of the chief values of the dance that it gives its girlish pupils such ideal training in this delicate strategy. For if the battle of Waterloo was won on the playing-fields of Eton, the battle of wedlock is won in the ball-rooms of Society.

Now, just as the procession has finished streaming into the ball-room, it begins streaming out again in animated, hungry couples. It feels that it has conscientiously completed all the preliminary work for the coming business of the night, and has deserved the rest and refreshment awaiting it at the supper-tables below. As it reaches the rooms in which the supper is to be consumed it splits up at the many tables into parties of six, eight, or ten. There are a good many of the men who, some from ill-luck, but the majority from choice, find themselves without supper partners. These organize "stag" tables, and have the bad taste to comport themselves with such evident enjoyment that many men, enthroned between grace and beauty, cast glances full of envy at these merry misogynists, while the ladies' regard is cold and stern at this tactless proof of feminine dispensability. There are, too, some girls who fail to secure

REST AND REFRESHMENT AWAIT AT THE
SUPPER-TABLE BELOW

partners. Of these the majority, exerting that mysterious power by which the snake gets itself fed by the most reluctant bird, and the woman gets herself proposed to by the most recalcitrant man, possess themselves at the last moment of companions for supper. But a few are left irretrievably without escorts. These poor victims of their sex cannot, like the men, form tables of their own. All that each can do is to disappear as swiftly and as secretly as possible, hurrying home in humiliation for the present and despair for the future. These are some of the little tragedies by which pathos can thrust its way into the most frivolous environment, to keep it flesh and blood. For humanity can exist without humor, but without pathos even beasts could not endure.

Supper is such a long, elaborate, and varied meal that a novice would probably conclude some catastrophe had suddenly overtaken the brace of orchestras or the ball-room floor, and that this was a Borgian wile of the hostess to place any further dancing hopelessly beyond the desires or capacities of her guests. If the supper were to be followed by an actual dance the results would indeed be calamitous. But it is to be followed by a cotillion, a system of entertainment in which the guests take their dancing on the instalment plan, and have time to rest between the watches.

At supper most of the women eat moderately and drink very sparingly, whether from scruples of conscience or of corsets is immaterial. Each of the men, however, toys with enough food to sustain a clerk for forty-eight hours, and sips enough champagne to send a day-laborer to the night court.

NEW YORK SOCIETY ON PARADE

The conversation which crackles through the rooms is at once animated and detached. Men and women address each other with the impersonal loquacity of barbers. Their attitude toward each other is much like their attitude toward the chauds-froids and the galantines which are set before them—familiarity with externals tempered by ignorance of contents.

After they have accomplished their uttermost the whole party wends its way back up the marble stairs considerably more slowly than it tripped down, hampered by an alliance of the laws of gravity and of gastronomy.

When the guests re-enter the ball-room they find the walls hedged by rows of light chairs, each of which is numbered. The young champion who is to lead the cotillion hands out to all the women slips of paper, on which are numbers corresponding with the chairs. In a land of equal opportunity it might be supposed that such a pillar of the Constitution as a cotillion would be conducted with malice toward none, with charity for all, with neither discrimination nor special privilege. But, alas! as the ladies seat themselves, a glance will show that to those who have has been given. Over each choicest post, over each strategic position, broods some corpulent coryphée, some withered bacchante, who has come to patronize and has stayed to pant. What are these poor ladies, patently the bugbears of a dancer, the nightmares of a lover, doing in such prominence? Ask the cotillion leader, and, if he be an honest young champion, he will whisper that these are persons of prestige who are certain to give dinners which he desires the distinction of eating, who are plotting cotillions which

AT SUPPER A SUPERFICIAL FAMILIARITY EXISTS

he craves the lustre of leading. So favoritism stalks, winking, even through these halls of exclusive equality, and only too often youthful grace and beauty despairingly take a back seat, while unlovely influence and affluence puff and perspire in the van.

Perhaps it is a pessimism induced by such unfairness that drives a number of men out of the glittering ball-room into the dimmer stateliness of the library, where the books are kept securely closed and the bottles invitingly open. Scotch, rye, champagne, are the favorite masterpieces standing in their glossy glass bindings, telling their stories in serial form, each chapter in a bumper, and each to be continued in our next. Here is the sanctum of the host. Here once a year he takes his place to dispense the only kind of hospitality within his grasp.

Highly starched and stupid, with a well-valeted body and an untended mind, full of misinformation and unassimilated alcohol, he sits, a long glass of "Scotch and carbonic" resting between his fingers on the broad arm of his chair, a fat black cigar between his fat red lips, a good-natured smile on his florid, flabby face. Occasionally he makes a sortie into the ball-room, insures his presence there being noted by his wife, and then hastily retreats into the library once more, where he takes a fresh highball, lights a new cigar, and throws himself didactically into any conversation that may be going on, with a bland confidence in the authority of his own ignorance. And he is largely justified, for his guests feel that a man whose wines are so sound cannot be far amiss in his ideas, and swallow them both, inextricably intermingled.

Throughout the night the library remains crowded with men enjoying the dance. Some are transients recurring at frequent intervals, seeking relief from the ball-room. Some sit permanent, immovable, glass in fist, cigar in mouth, talking gravely, talking lightly, taking no more interest in the strains of waltz or two-step than the dancers of the cotillion themselves.

These, sitting in two rows round the quadrangle of polished floor, are devoting themselves assiduously to the duties of the evening.

The young champion is leading the dance with the married daughter of the hostess. Together they walk over to a flowered recess at one side of the room. Willing hands from within the recess load them with gifts. They then start round the room in opposite directions, the leader distributing these favors to a certain number of the ladies, and the daughter of the house presenting them to an equal number of men. Then, to the sweet strains of the orchestra, each possessor of a favor minces across the slippery floor and bestows it upon a desired partner. The purchase price having been paid, they droop languidly into each other's arms and begin to dance.

At this moment, surely, the dance must justify itself, thinks a naïve footman pouring iced punch in the corner. Here is a girl in the full flush of her glorious youth who has just received a valuable present in jewelry from a young man, evidently given for the pure pleasure of a dance with her. They have a clear floor, a magnificent orchestra, an admiring audience: they have every opportunity to sate that passion for the dance which must have brought them to the ball. But what is this? They have scarcely swayed into the full rhythm of the waltz when the leader claps his white-gloved hands, and they and the other dancers halt and straightway return to their seats. Does the young man look furiously angered or the young woman coyly disappointed? The puzzled footman can see no such expressions. On the contrary, the young woman wears a delicate smile of gratification at having got hold of the favor for so little exertion, while the young man wears a well-bred grin of relief at having got rid of the favor in time to pay a quick trip to the library before the next figure. And if the footman, the next morning, prevails on the butler to expound this mystery to him, he will surely scratch his head at a singular state of affairs. It will appear that a remarkable number of the ladies and gentlemen do not take part in the cotillion for that love of dancing shown by some of those young ladies who have just been making their début into society, and by some of those gentlemen who have just been making theirs from the library. Most of the other gentlemen give their favors to the ladies not for the sake of the present dance, but of the future dinner. They select them not for the delectation which they arouse, but for the invitations which they command. They bore themselves with a dance that they may be entertained at a ball, they endure the monotonous melodies of the orchestra that they may attend the monotonous harmonies of the opera. They waltz for "week-ends," and two-step for yachting parties. They are no frivolous idlers, but ambitious men, working doggedly to achieve their goals. Nor are the majority of the ladies crude enough to welcome these gentlemen for their pretty looks, for their polished dancing, for their wise brains, their witty tongues, or their loving hearts. All that each yearns for is to have more partners and more favors than any of her friends. To her wide perspective these partners have no more individuality than does each grouse that falls to the sportsman's gun. They are merely partners, and every new one but adds to the number of brace that she can finally count as her evening's "bag." Lumpish or limping, wheezing or weltering, rake or relic, babe or blackguard, she grasps their favors and lapses into their embraces in the sexless safety of utter impersonality. At the end of the evening she certainly could not identify her various favors by the men who had given them, although she might be able to identify some few of the men by the most valuable favors. For though the men mean nothing to her, the favors mean everything. Her partners she values largely for the negative pleasure of keeping them away from her sisters, but the favors that they bring yield her the positive joy of acquisition and possession. To her, no matter what her age or ugliness, they are the trophies of her seduction, the spoils of her charms. For deep within her the natural woman, in her death throes, plays her this last pitiful prank of making her believe that every attention paid her is extracted by her own personal alluringness. She may fully realize and take pride in her position, her wealth, her influence; she may dimly realize and take shame in her wrinkles, her fat, her halting conversation. Yet if the most notorious sycophant pays her the courtesy of a favor, she will live and die in the secret conviction that it was paid because of what she was to him, not because of what she could do for him. But the ladies go a step further than this. Besides valuing the favors as symbols of their popularity, they prize them for their own intrinsic value. The more costly the favor the keener in gentle bosoms will be the pangs of emulation to secure it. They are, of course, supposed to be but sentimental souvenirs of the night's simple pleasures; and yet the more the souvenir costs, the more tender will be the sentiment associated with it. It seems curious to our friend, the naïve footman, to see women who own horses, houses, husbands, motors, and jewels worth millions, graduating their cupidity according to twenty-dollar differences between the favors' values. Yet it is a natural instinct, consistent with the principles of plutocracy, that nothing can be praised before being appraised, prized before being priced, or deprecated before being depreciated. It is for this reason that the woman owning miles of greenhouses will set more store on a gift of costly orchids than of fragrant violets, that she will appreciate a poor dinner of dishes expensively out of season more than an admirably cooked sequence of normal courses; that she will prefer at a musicale to hear songs by an exorbitant star with a cold in his head to the singing of a more modest artist in perfect voice. She belongs to a Society which has performed the feat of lifting itself off the ground by its own purse-strings. Why should not costliness be her criterion of life?

But now the footman's bewildered gaze lights on one couple, clings to them in pleasure and relief throughout the evolutions of the dance, and follows them tenaciously to their respective seats, when their brief turn is done. They sit at opposite ends of the room, both with partners of their own. But each time the young gentleman is given a favor to dispose of he speeds, as straight as arrow's flight, for this particular young lady. And twice, when the favors are hers to give, she aimlessly flits toward points six or seven chairs away from his, but is able to find no available recipient till she has come to him. She is not so brilliant or so beautiful as some other women here to-night, he is not so tall or handsome as some other men; but their path together seems like a soft golden thread gleaming through the harsh weavings of the dance. They tell a story which the footman can understand, tell it in words more subtle and more delicate than he himself could ever use in making such a story of his own, but words none the less so clear to him that, with a tender smile, he follows the couple's fortunes through the night, and pours punch very absent-mindedly.

In the mean time the dance continues, becoming each moment more whole-heartedly expensive and enjoyable. Its votaries in the library swarm thicker and thicker in the murk of cigar smoke. Champagne-bottles rise into sight and disappear like one of their own golden bubbles. Their contents swirl in foaming cataracts down thirsty throats to freshen weary bodies and irrigate parched minds. The host has lost much of his starch but none of his stupidity. Men stand and sit about with flabby, saturated shirt-fronts and clammy pendent collars, their faces flushed, their eyes bright, their tongues quickening, their affection and esteem for one another momentarily increasing. They beam with the relief of truancy. Amid the pleasures of stimulation and recuperation they feel gloriously at their ease. Every now and then one of more sensitive conscientiousness than the rest hears, in the distant crooning of the orchestra, the siren call of duty, and, gathering himself together, marches forth, a worthy son of Adam, to resume earning if not eating his sweetbreads in the sweat of his face.

In the ball-room the hostess's distribution of largess has become more and more handsome. Starting with pretty trinkets that one could pick up anywhere for five dollars, her two almoners are now lavishing articles of real value on the guests—gold match-safes, jewelled scarf-pins, lace sachets, hand-painted fans, silver picture-frames and cigar-cases become their personal property in quick succession. The men, in an ecstasy of chivalry or champagne, bestow on the ladies not only the favors intended for them, but also their own favors with which they have just been presented. Those women who are popular for their beauty and their charms, and those who are populous for their position and their prestige, sit—when they are allowed to sit at all—amid miniature mountains of loot, while even the less fortunate of their sisters have acquired tidy little collections of precious odds and ends. The former sit in unfeigned carelessness, knowing, with the arrogance of fortune's favorites, that each distribution of gifts will bring them offers of more than they can possibly dance into their possession. The latter sit with even greater carelessness of manner, each chatting and smiling to her partner, languidly fanning herself. But who will ever realize with what agonized suspense she watches the approach of every present-bearing male; with what wildly growing hopes she notes his course narrowing itself till it must surely be steered for her alone; with what boilings of fury beneath her placid, powdered bosom she sees him suddenly, treacherously tack when he is almost in her arms, and add his contribution to the treasures of the grinning beldame to her left? She goes on obliviously chatting and smiling to her partner, she goes on languidly fanning herself, but in her heart curdles the stuff that tragedies are made of. And tragedies do happen, not of violence, but of miserable sordidness. For the temptings of inflamed avarice and the promptings of wounded vanity are too strong a combination for some few women to withstand, and when they take their leave at the evening's end they carry amid their favors many which some other women, with unpleasant smiles, have missed from their belongings.

And now the cotillion has reached its last figure. The hostess's daughter encircles the room, handing out the final and most sumptuous donations. The favors are interchanged, the dancers take a few preparatory glides, catch the swing of the music, and waltz away, thanking each other profusely for the pleasant cotillion their hostess has given them. Gradually the dancing dies away, little by little the room thins out, the guests trooping by the hostess expressing their appreciation of the beauties and the pleasures of the ball. She receives their thanks with equanimity, and watches them depart with the same aloofness with which she saw them come. They walk down the stairs, the women's partners helping them carry part of their favors until these are taken over by their maids. Then, with the proud consciousness of a night's work well and faithfully performed, they disappear into the outer darkness like dainty housebreakers reeling beneath their "swag."

The ball is now over. It has gone into the history of balls. The hostess feels that her duty to Society has been accomplished, her labors consummated. Her thoughts turn longingly to cool sheets, soft pillows, the broken slumbers that are at least better than unbroken waking. Her head aches; each false curl feels as if it were made of iron, her tiara as though it were cast of lead. She feels the wrinkles gnawing through their shroud of artificial smoothness, she feels the skin collapse into sagging folds and pouches. She pulls herself together, and, with a dreadful effort, smiles as the young leader of her cotillion bustles up to say good-night. He congratulates her on the success of her entertainment, shakes hands with her and her daughter, and hurries away with the complacent air of the doctor who is able to say that he thinks mother and child will now do nicely.

The hostess turns to her daughter, who is standing waiting fretfully next her, and leaving her on this monotonous scene of well-won triumph, drags herself proudly like a wounded lioness to the elevator that will take her to her lair.

What is now left? It is four o'clock in the morning; the cotillion is over; its beneficiaries have for an hour past been departing with their profits; its leader has left; the hostess is yawning in the hands of her maid. Why are the lights still blazing, why is the orchestra still playing in the ball-room, why is a coterie of haggard maids still sitting in the entrance-hall, why are rows of black coats and silk hats still hanging, like modish scarecrows, in the men's cloak-room? Because at last the dance has triumphed over the ball, the long night's moment of vindication has come, pleasure has wormed itself free from artifice, and swirls in exultation round the room. In the hearts of a little band of men and women Nature has outlived the desolate hours of fevered ceremony, and now gives them her fresh and fervent thanks. The orchestra cease to be cynical and jaded artists, and become fiddlers, fiddling for them merrily; the floor slides smoothly underneath their winged feet, their bodies swing sinuously through the throbbing, flower-scented air; the zest of the dewless winter's dawn stings in their veins. Theirs is a free, uncrippled dance, of unthought figures, of unbought favors, the spontaneous pairing of men and women for unpremeditated pleasure in each other, to share with one another the harmony of music and of motion, which, like the greater harmony of love and life, never yields its pleasures to solitary selfishness, but must be shared to be possessed.

Thus they dance out of the night, through the dawn, on toward the sunrise, smiled on unwearyingly by the Great Hostess who is always brilliant and never snobbish, who is tolerant of everything but artifice and affectation, that eternal woman of the world whose hospitality men call Life.

THE END

THE LEISURE CLASS IN AMERICA

An Arno Press Collection

Bradley, Hugh. **Such was Saratoga.** 1940

Browne, Junius Henri. **The Great Metropolis:** A Mirror of New York. 1869

Burt, Nathaniel. **The Perennial Philadelphians.** 1963

Canby, Henry Seidel. **Alma Mater:** The Gothic Age of the American College. 1936

Crockett, Albert Stevens. **Peacocks on Parade.** 1931

Croffut, W[illiam] A. **The Vanderbilts.** 1886

Crowninshield, Francis W. **Manners for the Metropolis.** 1909

de Wolfe, Elsie. **The House in Good Taste.** 1913

Ellet, E[lizabeth] F[ries Lummis]. **The Court Circles of the Republic,** or The Beauties and Celebrities of the Nation. 1869

Elliott, Maud Howe. **This Was My Newport.** 1944

Elliott, Maud Howe. **Uncle Sam Ward and His Circle.** 1938

Fairfield, Francis Gerry. **The Clubs of New York** and Croly, [Jane C.] **Sorosis.** 1873/1886. Two vols. in one

[Fawcett, Edgar]. **The Buntling Ball:** A Graeco-American Play. 1885

Fawcett, Edgar. **Social Silhouettes.** 1885

Fiske, Stephen. **Off-Hand Portraits of Prominent New Yorkers.** 1884

Foraker, Julia B. **I Would Live It Again:** Memories of a Vivid Life. 1932

Goodwin, Maud Wilder. **The Colonial Cavalier.** 1895

Hartt, Rollin Lynde. **The People at Play.** 1909

Lehr, Elizabeth Drexel. **"King Lehr" and the Gilded Age.** 1935

Lodge, Henry Cabot. **Early Memories.** 1913

[Longchamp, Ferdinand]. **Asmodeus in New-York.** 1868

McAllister, [Samuel] Ward. **Society as I Have Found It.** 1890

McLean, Evalyn, with Boyden Sparkes. **Father Struck It Rich.** 1936

[Mann, William d'Alton]. **Fads and Fancies of Representative Americans at the Beginning of the Twentieth Century.** 1905

Martin, Frederick Townsend. **The Passing of the Idle Rich.** 1911

Martin, Frederick Townsend. **Things I Remember.** 1913

Maurice, Arthur Bartlett. **Fifth Avenue.** 1918

[Mordecai, Samuel]. **Richmond in By-Gone Days.** 1856

Morris, Lloyd. **Incredible New York.** 1951

Neville, Amelia Ransome. **The Fantastic City:** Memoirs of the Social and Romantic Life of Old San Francisco. 1932

Nichols, Charles Wilbur de Lyon. **The Ultra-Fashionable Peerage of America.** 1904

Pound, Arthur. **The Golden Earth:** The Story of Manhattan's Landed Wealth. 1935

Pulitzer, Ralph. **New York Society on Parade.** 1910

Ripley, Eliza. **Social Life in Old New Orleans.** 1912

Ross, Ishbel. **Silhouette in Diamonds:** The Life of Mrs. Potter Palmer. 1960

Sherwood, M[ary] E[lizabeth W.]. **Manners and Social Usages.** 1897

The Sporting Set. 1975

Van Rensselaer, [May] King. **Newport: Our Social Capital.** 1905

Van Rensselaer, [May] King. **The Social Ladder.** 1924

Wharton, Edith and Ogden Codman, Jr. **The Decoration of Houses.** 1914

Williamson, Jefferson. **The American Hotel.** 1930